D1243445

The Wild West in American History

SCOUTS

Written by Gail Stewart
Illustrated by Tom Casmer/Spectrum Studios
Edited by Mark E. Ahlstrom

LIBRARY OF CONGRESS
Library of Congress Cataloging-in-Publication Data

Stewart, Gail, 1949-
   Scouts / Gail B. Stewart.
     p. cm. -- (The Wild West in American history)
   Summary: Describes the activities of the scouts who guided soldiers
and new travelers through the western frontier in the nineteenth century.
   ISBN 0-86625-404-8
   1. Scouts and scouting--West (U.S.)--History--19th century--Juvenile
literature. 2. Frontier and pioneer life--West (U.S.)--Juvenile literature.
3. West (U.S.)--Description and travel--To 1848--Juvenile literature.
[1. Scouts and scouting--West (U.S.) 2. Frontier and pioneer life--West
(U.S.) 3. West (U.S.)]   I. Title. II. Series.
F592.S793 1990
978' .02--dc20   89-37210
                                        CIP
                                        AC

Rourke Publications, Inc.
Vero Beach, Florida, 32964

SCOUTS

SCOUTS

Some people called them "guides." Others called them "scouts." Whatever the name, they were the ones who could lead a wagon train through the wilderness. They could find a trail through friendly Indian territory, and avoid encounters with hostile tribes.

The U.S. Army needed these scouts. Cavalry units had recently come west to protect the new settlers. The officers and men didn't know the area any better than the settlers did. One cavalry officer claimed that his scouts were more valuable to him than gold. "I know as surely as I know my name that without these brave guides, thousands of officers would have been killed or lost. When our troops were in danger of starving because there was no game, our scouts fed us. They are canny to the ways of this wild country. How much of a difference our guides have made to the U.S. Army!"

A historian who wrote about the West said that without the scouts, America would not have moved west until the 20th century. There were so many dangers, and so many ways travelers could get into trouble. A wrong turn could mean injury or death, not to mention lots of wasted time. No matter how brave the explorers, or how dedicated the pioneers, it was the scouts who led the way through the mountains and the forests.

IN THE BEGINNING

What is now the western United States has changed drastically since 1840. Before there were cities and towns, there were only small, roughly built settlements. Before the little settlements, there were only Native American villages scattered throughout the West.

The first non-Indians to visit the area were trappers and traders. Coming mostly from France and England, these men found the streams and rivers of the West swarming with beavers. The beaver was almost worth its weight in gold back then. Wealthy people were wearing hats made of beaver felt. The hatmakers in New York and throughout Europe were eager to buy all the beaver pelts the traders and trappers could get.

As the years went by, there were more Americans doing the trapping and trading. From St. Louis and other places they would come, heading west toward the Rocky Mountains, or "Shining Mountains," as they called them. Many of these trappers and traders became used to the rough wilderness. They preferred living without the luxuries of cities and towns, and enjoyed the solitude. These are the people who became known as "mountain men."

The mountain men were skilled survivors in a very dangerous world. They faced hazards everywhere—from grizzly bears and mountain lions to blinding snowstorms and hostile Indian tribes. The mountain men had to be both lucky and smart to stay alive!

By 1840, however, fashion had changed. People were no longer buying beaver hats as they had been. The new style was a hat of Chinese silk. The hatmakers had little use for beaver pelts, so most traders and trappers were out of a job.

Some of these men headed back to St. Louis. Some became businessmen; others started farming. For most of the mountain men, however, returning to the city was unthinkable. The wilderness may have been dangerous, but it was better than being cooped up in civilization, they thought. Many of the mountain men decided to keep on with their trapping, earning just enough of a living to get by.

Before white settlers came, Native Americans—like these Crow warriors—lived throughout the western United States. (Photo: University of Oklahoma.)

A NATION MOVING WEST

At the same time many trappers were heading back east, many other Americans were heading west. Some wanted to explore the vast section of the country about which they had heard stories. Some wanted to settle down and raise their families in the wilderness. They were excited by the idea of living in a new land.

Some of the people were missionaries, interested in spreading their religion to the Native Americans. Some were scientists and mapmakers. Some were naturalists, who wanted to learn about the many new species of animals and plants in the West.

As time went on, there were also railroad builders, interested in connecting the cities and towns of the East with the West. There were also soldiers—cavalrymen whose job it was to keep the civilians safe from the danger of Indian raids.

Back in 1840 it was a complicated thing to move west. There were no roads or campgrounds. There were no places to stop

along the way to eat or shop for essentials. The only paths were a few areas worn down by Indian ponies and buffalo herds. A map of the West did not exist.

The only people besides the Indians who knew the area were the trappers and traders. They had much of the West "mapped" in their heads. The new travelers needed help finding their way through this territory, and they turned to the mountain men. These mountain men became the scouts who led the settlers into the new land.

Millions of buffalo once roamed the western plains of the United States.

"OUR EYES AND EARS"

One woman who traveled west in a wagon train kept a daily journal. She wrote about the day-to-day routine of life in a covered wagon. Although there were plenty of scary and exciting adventures that she and her family had

This old drawing shows a scout leading
a wagon train across the plains.
(Photo: Oregon Historical Society.)

during their long journey, she spent much of her time writing about the scouts. She wrote that the wagon-train scouts were the "eyes and ears" of the travelers. What did she mean by that?

For one thing, the scouts had lived for years in the territory. They understood the weather, the dangers, and the lay of the land. If something looked suspicious or odd to the scout, he would alert the travelers so they could defend themselves.

The scouts could also "read signs." That meant that they could look closely at the ground and tell who or what had been there before. Every leaf, every blade of grass could tell a story to a

sharp-eyed scout. In one case, a wagon train came upon a large pile of horse droppings. The travelers were afraid that the horse droppings were a sign that the Indians were nearby.

The scout didn't even need to get off his horse to look at the droppings. He could tell at a glance that there was nothing to fear. He explained to the wagon master that the droppings were probably made by wild horses, not Indian ponies. The reason the scout knew

that, he explained, was that a horse that is being ridden does not stop to leave droppings. Their droppings would be scattered. Wild horses, on the other hand, stop whenever they feel like eating grass.

So even things that may have seemed unimportant to most people were clues. A good scout had to be able to "read signs" such as these. His understanding of such things frequently saved lives.

THE INDIAN WAYS

Scouts taught the settlers many useful things they had learned from Native Americans—like protecting horses' hooves by binding them with buffalo hide.

*M*any of these scouts had lived among Indians back in their trapping days. They had a deep respect for the Native American's ability to survive. Much of what the scouts knew had been taught to them by Indians.

For instance, one party of travelers wanted to avoid being followed. They were nervous about a tribe of Blackfoot Indians that had threatened to steal their horses. The scout knew an Indian trick. He had the travelers ride their horses through the shallow water of a river. This way, no one could follow their trail.

Another time, a group of explorers was journeying west through the mountains. The ground was jagged and rocky, and the horses had worn through their horseshoes. The explorers didn't want to hurt their horses' feet. The scout, who had lived among the Crow Indians in his trapping days, showed them how to wrap the horses' hooves in buffalo hide. The thick buffalo skin protected the horses' bruised and tender feet along the rocky trail.

Many of the westward travelers in the 19th century had never seen a Native American. They had only heard stories about Indians from other travelers. Many people thought of Indians not as people, but as just another danger in the wilderness. They considered the Indians to be savages—bloodthirsty warriors who were just waiting for a chance to murder and scalp white travelers.

The scouts knew that this kind of thinking was wrong. They also knew that it was dangerous. Thinking that all Indians were enemies, the travelers were fearful. They were ready to shoot any Indian they saw approaching their camp. The history of the American West is filled with sad stories of what happened when people shot first and asked questions later. Many of the Indians who were shot by nervous white travelers weren't planning an attack. Many were approaching the camp to trade. Others were just curious about the reason for the white men's journey west.

But the result of such thoughtless action was usually the same. The camp would often be attacked by other Indians, who were angry about the shooting of their tribesman. There would be more shooting, and more killing. These battles led to more mistrust and more hatred on both sides.

"WE SPOKE NO INDIAN"

A man traveling west in 1843 wrote in his journal that he hoped he never had to meet an Indian. "I was certain that there are some honorable men among them," he wrote. "However, we knew that they spoke only to one another, and as far as those in our party— we spoke no Indian."

This man obviously didn't know much about American Indians. Each tribe had its own language—the Crow tribe spoke a language different from that of the Blackfeet. Indians were no more alike in language and culture than, say, French and Russians were.

There were hundreds of different languages spoken by American Indian tribes in the 19th century. Not only were there differences among tribes, but there were also variations among villages of the same tribe. For instance, a village of Crow Indians living on one side of a river might pronounce their words a bit differently from people in a Crow village across the river 30 miles away. It would be almost impossible for anyone—Indian or non-Indian—to learn all those languages!

USING YOUR HANDS

Jim Bridger was one of the most famous of all the scouts. Like most of the others, Bridger had been a mountain man for many years. He had many friends among the Indians, and was able to speak five or six different Indian languages.

Bridger was also able to communicate with any Native American he met, because he knew sign language. This special sign language was first used by Indians of various tribes to speak with one another. It was made up of hand signals that were fairly easy to understand, and easy to learn. For example, the sign for "a liar" was to put two fingers by the tongue, to show that someone was using a double meaning. The expression in the eyes and the set of the mouth were important in this sign language, too.

When Bridger encountered an Indian

Using his hands, a scout "talks" to the leader of a group of Native Americans.

messenger, he would try to establish communication right away. Often the messenger would want the scout to meet with his chief. Bridger and the chief would sit down around a campfire, perhaps with others in the tribe, and silently "discuss" their business in sign language. These discussions were usually quite lively. Bridger had quite a sense of humor, and enjoyed using sign language to tell funny stories to the Indians he met. There would often be several minutes of silence. Then fingers would fly, and there would be lots of gesturing. Usually there would be loud hoots of laughter from the Indians. They seemed to enjoy Bridger's silent jokes!

Jim Bridger was a master of sign language.
(Photo: University of Oklahoma.)

The settlers were cooking their evening meal when the scout noticed danger in the distance.

QUICK THINKING SAVES LIVES

There were plenty of times on the trail when a scout had to make decisions quickly. Lives often depended on a fast and accurate response.

In one instance, a wagon train heading to California was camped for the night. Most of the people were busily working, gathering firewood, and preparing the evening meal. Although nothing seemed wrong, the scout was nervous.

Something was odd. There appeared to be a dust storm off in the distance, perhaps 20 miles away. There was no wind, though. He scanned the horizon, looking for other signs of a storm, but there was nothing.

After several minutes, the scout knew what was making the far-away dust storm. A gigantic herd of buffalo—maybe as many as a thousand of the animals—was stampeding across the plains. Something had set them off, and they were blindly charging toward the wagon train. The buffalo would trample anything in their path—they would certainly crush the people and their wagons. The stampede still looked to be many miles away, but the dust from their hooves was plainly visible. There was no time to lose!

The scout raced back to the campsite and yelled to the people to build huge fires—as big as they possibly could. The travelers looked puzzled. The small cooking fire they had started was enough to make their supper. The evening wasn't cold enough to need a fire for warmth. They wondered why they needed more fires.

The scout had no time to explain. He grabbed an armful of the extra fire wood, and threw it several yards in front of one of the wagons. He yelled at some of the others to do the same. As he worked, he explained that buffalo, like most other animals, are naturally afraid of fire. If the party got a string of large fires going, he said, there was a chance the stampede would veer off to one side. If not, they were all as good as dead.

Needless to say, the people hurriedly built the fires, adding some of their precious belongings to the blazes to make them even bigger. They watched in awe as the stampeding herd drew closer and closer. They could see the animals now, shaggy and wild-eyed. There was nowhere to run, since the herd was several hundred yards wide. There was a deadening rumble, which must have sounded like one of our large jets taking off. There were tons of dirt and dust in the air. It appeared as if the buffalo didn't even see the fires. At the last second, however, the animals swerved.

The travelers' horses snorted and reared, terrified as the ground shook beneath them. One of the travelers later wrote that although he had never felt the power of an earthquake, he knew it could not be much different from the feeling of those animals crashing across the plains.

Weak-kneed and frightened, the travelers were safe. They had lost a few of their belongings to the fires, but their lives had been saved by a quick-thinking scout.

The terrified settlers pray that their fires will turn the herd of buffalo.

MANY WAYS OF BEING SMART

Those who have studied the scouts agree on one thing—they were physically remarkable. They were strong and quite healthy. Rheumatism, a condition of the muscles and joints that makes them stiff and achy, was about the only complaint the scouts had. Their rheumatism was probably not a result of their scouting. Rather, it probably came from their trapping days—from wading in icy mountain streams and sleeping in cold, damp clothes.

The scouts also had great powers of concentration. Their hearing had to be good. And their vision—well, that was legendary. Jim Bridger supposedly had the best eyes in the country. It was said that he could see rock formations and other landmarks 50 miles away! When he pointed such things out to his fellow travelers, they just shook their heads. No, they didn't see whatever he was pointing to. Bridger was irritated by what he called their "poor vision." It wasn't until the party had traveled 20 or 30 more miles that the landmarks became visible—barely—to the rest of the travelers!

Although their physical abilities were all superb, the scouts were different in their intelligence. There were many ways of being a smart scout.

Take Jim Bridger, for example. He could not have passed a third grade spelling test. He could barely write his own name. He never learned to read. Yet he was one of the smartest scouts who ever lived.

What made him so smart? For one thing, Bridger had what is called a photographic memory. That means that after seeing something just once, he would remember it. A mountain, a clump of trees, or a little path through the hills—Bridger could recollect them all. This was extremely valuable for a scout, because other people were counting on him to guide them through unfamiliar territory. Bridger was like a human map, and the best one in existence for many years. While some of the early printed maps of the West had errors, Bridger's memory did not!

Bridger was also a master of remembering what he heard. This made it easy for him to learn new Indian languages. He could also repeat any story or message word for word as it had been told to him. This ability made him an excellent storyteller, for he had hundreds of tales from which to choose. There is a true story about Jim Bridger that shows just how good this "listening memory" was.

Once when Bridger was scouting for a wagon

train, he was talking to one of the travelers. The man complimented Bridger on his storytelling ability.

"Do you know who was supposed to be the best storyteller in history?" asked the man.

Bridger did not.

"It was a fellow named William Shakespeare," said the man. "Everybody says he was the best."

Bridger's curiosity was aroused. If there was one thing he admired, it was the ability to spin a good yarn. The man told him that many of Shakespeare's "yarns" were written down in a large book. Bridger then rode from wagon to wagon, asking whether anyone was carrying this volume of Shakespeare. He finally located a copy, and made arrangements to borrow it.

Because Bridger couldn't read, he hired one of the children in the wagon train to read to him each night. After a few weeks on the journey, Bridger had heard some of Shakespeare's most famous plays—*Macbeth*, *Hamlet*, and others. As always, he was able to remember most of them almost word for word. (Those who listened to Bridger reciting Shakespeare around a campfire did say that he added a few colorful "mountain man" words of his own!)

Night after night, a young settler read Shakespeare's famous plays to Jim Bridger.

"A GIANT OF A MAN"

Another way of being smart is to know when to keep your mouth shut. Some call it "tact," or "diplomacy." Simply put, it is the ability to make a suggestion without offending other people. It came in very handy for scouts of the Old West.

There would often be times when the leader of the travelers or explorers would have a plan in mind. The plan might be a good one, or it might have serious flaws. The scout might recognize that the plan was dangerous or foolish. But what should he say? Many of the men a scout worked for were very important, respected

people. They were proud of their abilities, and didn't appreciate a scout contradicting their orders. In cases such as these, a scout really needed some of that diplomacy!

Christopher "Kit" Carson was one of the most famous scouts of the Old West. He was very small—only 5 feet 4 inches tall. Yet those who watched him work said he was "a giant of a man." He was an excellent "sign" reader, a fearless fighter, and a master of tact and diplomacy. He was not a leader, and didn't feel comfortable shouting orders at others. Instead, he quietly made suggestions to his superiors,

The desert west of the Great Salt Lake had never been crossed.

and tried to go along with their orders whenever possible.

Carson's most famous boss was an explorer named John Fremont. Fremont was a lieutenant in the U.S. Army Corps of Engineers in the mid-1800's. He was anxious to explore several parts of the West.

Carson's job was to make sure that John Fremont's enthusiasm didn't get them killed. Fremont was eager to explore territory not yet

John Fremont was known as "The Pathfinder." *(Photo: Oregon Historical Society.)*

"Kit" Carson became known as "The Pathfinder's Pathfinder." *(Photo: University of Oklahoma.)*

seen by others. Although he was usually a thoughtful and careful planner, he sometimes overlooked common sense and safety.

In one instance, Fremont wanted to cross a hot, dry area of land west of the Great Salt Lake. This desert hadn't been crossed before. Even the Native Americans who lived nearby avoided it. Some of the men in the explorer's party were reluctant. What about water? Surely they and their horses couldn't survive in that desert!

Carson knew Fremont was stubborn about this trip. He didn't try to talk Fremont out of it. Instead, he suggested that a small band of men should go first, before the others. If they found the going too rough, they could return to the main party.

Fremont agreed, and sent Carson and three

other men into the desert. They traveled in the evening hours, when it was cool. The small party went more than 60 miles without seeing water or vegetation. Finally, they reached mountains that had grass for the horses and firewood for their campfires. Best of all, there were several cold mountain streams. Carson and his men immediately built a fire and sent smoke signals—Indian style—to Fremont.

Over the years, Fremont became quite famous, as his expeditions in the West opened more and more territory. He became known as "The Pathfinder." But Fremont and his men gave much credit to their scout, Kit Carson, whom they called "The Pathfinder's Pathfinder."

Carson sends smoke signals to Fremont.

"HATLESS" CHARLEY

The danger that Kit Carson and his party faced, that of running out of water, was a very real threat to many travelers in the Old West. Charley Reynolds, a scout for the U.S. Army, almost died of thirst when carrying an important message back to headquarters.

"Headquarters" was Fort Laramie, more than 120 miles southwest of where Reynolds and a cavalry platoon were camped. The route was dangerous, because it was through territory inhabited by Sioux Indians. The Sioux were angry at the army's invasion of their hunting lands. It was vital that the message be delivered, but because of the risks, no one volunteered. At last, Charley Reynolds stepped forward.

The Sioux were known for their skill in tracking down their enemies. Reynolds knew he would have to be both smart and lucky to get through to Laramie. One of the first things he did in preparing for the journey was to cover his horse's feet with little leather boots. The boots would cover the horseshoes, thereby disguising the tracks. Indians never nailed metal horseshoes on their animals, and he wanted to make the Sioux think his horse was an Indian pony.

Charley Reynolds dressed like an Indian to fool his pursuers.

This old drawing shows Fort Laramie as it appeared at the time of Charley Reynold's adventure. *(Photo: Oregon Historical Society.)*

**Reynolds hid during the day
and traveled at night.**

The journey proved to be a nightmare. Reynolds traveled at night, to avoid being seen. Unfortunately, the route he took was very short on water. Day after day, each spot he had to camp was almost without water. Even the creek beds he came across held just a few puddles.

By the third day, historians tell us, Reynolds was weak and dizzy. His mouth was like cotton, and his tongue was almost twice its normal size from a lack of water. He led his horse rather than riding it, because the animal was suffering, too. Not wanting to be seen during the day, Reynolds would hide himself and his horse in shallow caves. He quietly crawled on his hands and knees from his hiding places, gathering handfuls of grass for his horse.

Reynolds knew he was dangerously close to death. He decided to take a really desperate gamble. Removing his hat and throwing aside his saddle, Reynolds mounted his tired horse. He simply had to make better time, and if he rode hard for a few hours, he might find water. The idea behind removing the saddle and his hat was a trick. He was sure he'd seen Sioux scouting parties. From a distance, a hatless man riding bareback on a pony would look like an Indian. White men never traveled without a hat—they weren't accustomed to the hot sun.

The plan worked, even though Reynolds saw several Sioux. They glanced at him, but never bothered him. With his bare head and tan skin, he must have looked like an Indian from a distance. Although many pounds lighter, and almost delirious from lack of water, Reynolds delivered the message to Fort Laramie.

INDIAN SCOUTS

*I*t would be wrong to give the impression that all the scouts of the Old West were white men. They certainly were not. In fact, there were far more Indians than whites employed as scouts. Historians tell us that in all, there were fewer than 40 white scouts in the Old West. The Indian numbers were far higher.

In 1866, Congress passed a law allowing President Andrew Johnson to hire 1,000 Native Americans as scouts. Most of the work of these scouts was to help make the western territories safe for white settlers. In some cases, they would be armed guards, protecting crews constructing railroads. In all cases, these Indian scouts would be used for fighting hostile Indian tribes.

It is hard for some people to understand how Indians could have helped kill other Indians. Those who have studied the Indians and the Old West say there are reasons that Indians became scouts for white settlers and the army. The Indians did not think of themselves as belonging to one large group. Each tribe, as we have mentioned, had its own language. Tribes also had their own customs and ways of doing things. Often, these differences led to fighting between tribes. For centuries before the first white settlers came to America, there had been bloody wars—Pawnee against Cherokee, Cheyenne against Apache. Many Indians hated other tribes more than the white settlers.

Scouting appealed to Indians for other reasons. Some saw the job as a way to earn money. Others were anxious to get off the new reservations. They were proud of their abilities to track and "read signs," and scouting gave them those opportunities.

In many cases, Indian scouts were able to avoid violent showdowns between the army and Indian tribes. The scouts could appeal to the Indians, and reason with them in ways the Indians could respect and understand.

THE END OF AN ERA

The need for scouts disappeared completely by the 1880's. The West was quickly being tamed. The paths made by

The Oregon-California Trail was one of the main routes West.

FT. DALLES

THE SCOUT

GREAT SALT LAKE

FT.

FT. CHURCHILL

the first scouts and their travelers had become roads. More and more people saw the West as a safe and exciting place to live. There was no longer a need for pathfinders.

What had once been a frontier changed into territories, and finally states. Native Americans had been driven onto reservations and were no longer a threat to the white settlers who took their lands.

Most of the scouts were old men by that time. They had led lives filled with more adventure than we can imagine. First as trappers, then as guides and scouts, these men made an important contribution to the growth of the United States. They were the eyes and ears of the movement westward.

After the 1880's, scenes like this were never repeated again. *(Photo: Oregon Historical Society)*

THE OREGON-CALIFORNIA TRAIL

DGER

FT. LARAMIE

COUNCIL BLUFFS

FT. KEARNY

INDEPENDENCE

SURVIVING IN A WILD LAND

Communicating with Native American tribes was only one part of a scout's job. Even when the nearby Indians were friendly, there were still many hazards that a scout had to look out for.

One of a scout's most important jobs was to make sure that his companions got enough to eat. For the travelers, it was a new land, with different types of animals and birds. The scout, on the other hand, had lived on his own in the West for many years. He knew the best places to hunt, and how to stalk game.

Usually a scout was successful in his hunting. He, and perhaps one or two of the travelers, would be able to shoot a deer, or even a buffalo. The meat would be roasted over a fire, and then the travelers would feast! There were usually no other parts to the meal. Meat, and maybe some bread, made up most of the traveler's diet.

Carrying a large cooking pot was awkward and cumbersome, so the scout often showed the travelers how to "make their own." He would take the large, thick stomach out of a freshly killed buffalo. It could be hung on sticks over the cooking fire and used as a portable pot. As long as it was kept moist, it wouldn't burn. After a few days, the "pot" would get stretched out and thin, and perhaps it would leak. When this happened, it was simply eaten! If the scout and his

party were lucky, they would shoot another buffalo and use its stomach in the same way.

As plentiful as game was in the West, many westward travelers and explorers died of starvation on their journeys. This may seem odd, because most of the time the woods and plains were full of game. There were times, though, when a scout would venture out looking for game and have no luck. There were some days when the game would seem to disappear. The woods and plains would appear empty.

In times like these, the scout had to come up with something else. Humans cannot go for too many days without food of some sort. People who are traveling need even more food. Walking, climbing, and driving the wagon's oxen or horses were all very strenuous work.

People who kept journals of their westward journeys tell all kinds of stories about the strange foods they had to eat, just to keep alive. They sometimes ate insects, such as crickets or grasshoppers. There have been many stories of scouts helping the travelers boil their leather moccasins. The shoes must have been tough, but at least there was some food value in them.

There were many times that a faithful dog had to be killed and eaten. At other times, some of the mules or pack horses had to be killed for food. This was a great hardship for the travelers. It meant that some of their belongings would have to be loaded onto other horses that were already loaded down. Sometimes the travelers would be forced to walk, using their riding horses to carry supplies. In many cases, heavy belongings had to be abandoned along the trail.

One survival trick that scouts used was to make a small cut in a horse's neck. The blood would be collected, and used to make a soup. This sounds awful, but it was a good trick for two reasons. First, the horse didn't need to be killed—and that was important to the travelers. The second reason was that the blood would provide enough nutrition for the travelers to go a few extra miles—perhaps to a place with better hunting.

One of a scout's biggest jobs was to feed the settlers.

IN THE DAYS OF THE SCOUTS

1809	Christopher "Kit" Carson is born in Kentucky.
1812	Louisiana becomes the 18th state.
1814	British troops set the White House and the Capitol building on fire.
1822	Clement Moore writes "A Visit From St. Nicholas," which begins: "'Twas the night before Christmas..."
1824	Mexico makes Texas one of its provinces.
1825	The Erie Canal opens.
1828	The Democratic Party is formed.
1831	Black Hawk, chief of the Fox and Sauk Indian nations, agrees to lead his people from their own land to a settlement west of the Mississippi River.
1832	Last rendezvous of the trappers and mountain men.
1837	Michigan becomes the 26th state.
1841	A scout named Thomas Fitzpatrick leads the first emigrant wagon train to the West Coast.
1842	Kit Carson scouts for John Fremont in the first of three exploratory missions.
1849	A stagecoach line opens between Independence, Missouri, and Santa Fe, New Mexico.
1850	The first sparrows are brought to America from England, in an effort to control the caterpillars.
1852	Roget's *Thesaurus* is published.
1857	Thomas Edison reads his first science book, then builds a chemistry lab in his basement.
1858	Teddy Roosevelt is born.
1859	The price of a field slave is $2,000.
1861	America's Civil War begins.
1865	President Abraham Lincoln is assassinated while watching a play in Washington, D.C.
1865	The Union Stockyards open in Chicago.
1870	The U.S. population is 38,558,371.
1874	The Republican Party adopts an elephant as its symbol.
1881	Jim Bridger dies on his farm in Missouri.